MW01482002

POET OF CHRIST:
WHISPERS OF FLOWERS

Psalms of Reverence by Morgan Bobbie St. Claire

FriesenPress

Suite 300 - 990 Fort St
Victoria, BC, Canada, V8V 3K2
www.friesenpress.com

ISBN
978-1-4602-6961-9 (Hardcover)
978-1-4602-6962-6 (Paperback)
978-1-4602-6963-3 (eBook)

1. Poetry, Subjects & Themes, Inspirational & Religious

Distributed to the trade by The Ingram Book Company

I wish to dedicate this book
Poet of Christ: Whispers of Flowers
To the memory of my Great-Grandmother,
Mrs. Elizabeth Brennan Saunders Simpson,
Who was a poet of gentleness and
Heartfelt love
To the residents of the Knox Church
In Medicine Hat, Alberta,
Where she would recite her Scottish poetry
to the goodly people
Of the church.

I would also like to dedicate this book
To Country Squire Villa
In Osoyoos, B.C.,
With affection.

Sincerely,
Morgan Bobbie St. Claire

Table of Contents

ACKNOWLEDGMENTS

I would like to thank the editor of my manuscript, as well as the designers of my book, at FriesenPress Publishing, for outstanding work and completion of a project that has been close to my heart. I would especially like to thank Galia Zavgorodni of FriesenPress for all her advice and continued support and encouragement that led to the publication of this book.

Also, I would like to thank Joanne Proctor, associate author of *You're Never Too Old to DREAM DARE DANCE! For every woman over 40;* by BERMUDA MEDIA, Published 2009, for her contribution of time in her role as computer teacher to myself.

I would like to thank the staff and citizens of Country Squire for being there to accept letters of my writings, which then became the poems of this book, *Poet of Christ: Whispers of Flowers.*

Sincerely,
Morgan Bobbie St. Claire

FOREWORD

Flowers and children are together in God's Garden, where the Master stands holding wild roses and where Mary stands with thousands of flowers to give to her children.

This book is called *Poet of Christ* because I am a lady and a scribe of the Eternal Christ. It is called *Whispers of Flowers* because it is a book of prayer to the Father, to Mary, and to Jesus.

I have said that I am a lady and a scribe of the Christ because of the visions I see, and because I have heard the thunder created by Saint Mary on October 26, 2014, in a miracle of the sun.

I feel the Passion of Jesus echo through my being, and I share this passion of Jesus and Saint Mary with the children who stand in God's Garden. As a scribe, this book is meant to generate a revealing of the Word in a poetic light with beauty and with the hint of a new warrior. It is with grace that I have offered my services as a scribe to Jesus and our beloved Mother, Mary.

My desire to touch the Sun has also been portrayed by what I have termed "a blossom of romance of the Arjuna" which is of Paramahansa Yogananda, a greatly beloved mystic and saint of India. May "His Nectar of the world," which flows like a river, be partaken of by the grace of the Holy Chalice by those of this age, and may the silver dragon send you to Heaven to know goodness, the silver dragon being a Caduceus—or Kundalini awakening, or the rod of Moses in the desert.

Sincerely,

Morgan Bobbie St. Claire

SAINT BERNADETA

May the Wings of Paradise
Take you on a Journey
To the Grotto of the Blessed Virgin
Where Saint Bernadeta stood
With mighty Angels around her,
"Hail Mary, full of grace."
With the words of the Lady being
"I am the Immaculate Conception."
Saint Bernadeta,
Visionary of Lourdes,
Felt religious ecstasies
And was a warrior of Christ
Throughout her sainted life.
The Victory of Lourdes,
"A Celebration of the Blessed!"
As Saint Bernadeta gave words of song
Like a psalmist of the Lord,
Who, herself,
Stood between two mountains
And as standing
Between two powerful mountains
Hence, in a valley
The Psalm of Bernadeta was heard
As a song.
The valley was
Her place of grace,
Which was, in truth,
A grotto.
Ave Maria! Hallelujah!

A GARDEN OF A PROPHET OF ISRAEL

The love I felt coursed throughout my soul,
And clung to wild flowers that were so loved
By God.
Through the taking of the Hyssop,
I declared myself a free person,
Ignoring the bitter herbs.
Throughout exodus, God was with me
While I did wear
Myrtle blossoms in my hair.
And from the Tamarisk Tree of the desert,
Which broke from the sky,
Then broke into crystals.
Like a child of Israel
I drank of its nectar.
I had a Temple of Worship
Called a Temple of Grace.
A Church in the centre of the sun
From whence I spun wild sage
To please the vision in my soul,
While almond blossoms became the
Precious thought to "become,"
And in becoming, I became liberated.
Being in the Promised Land,
I now became a warrior,

And the roses of Jericho bloomed pungently
While I was making a house out of Juniper.
And then came the time in the Desert of Judah
When I walked upon the crystals of the sand.
And all manner of daffodils and narcissus
And viburnum,
Grew all around me.

TO BRUCE, A POEM

Roses bloom at the hem of a blue robe
Where doves rest — at the feet of Mary.
A rosary falls with love
And with supplication,
As petals drift
From the light of Heaven
To the light of Earth.
From Mary's hands as a prayer.
May the glass rose you received at Christmas time
Be an embellishment of the rosary.
And remember
Wild roses grow on a mountain, too,
The wild mountains of Osoyoos,
Where you walk tall
And carry with you, maybe,
Paint and roses
So that your blessed heart becomes all well.
And my prayer to God is, Bruce,
When I touch the rosary
That your health will rise up like a silver dragon,
Climb all the way to Heaven,
And know goodness.

A LETTER TO BOB AND SHARON

May the Angels of the Highest Heavens
From the different light rays
Hold you in their arms
With the love of God.
May you be held in acclaim and obeisance
To the Sacred Heart of Jesus
And to the love of
The Sorrowful Immaculate Heart of Mary.
May the Son—
Who loves the Sun (who is the Father)—
And who loves his mother, Miriam,
Whom He honored throughout His life,
And who loves His
Virginal adoptive father, Joseph,
Whom He always listened to.
Bestow upon you both the love
Of the Nine Choir of Seraphim
And the sacred love of the Master Jesus
And the holy love of the Virgin Maiden, Mary.
May I offer you the love of my own heart
In all its purity and honesty,
To strike in you both
A chord
Of the music of Heaven.
May the honesty and the mettle of the cherished
Seek vigor in the adoration of Heaven.

THE ASCENSION OF AN ANGEL

May the ascension of an Angel
Upon the wings of cobalt fire
Take you on a journey to Israel.
There cobalt is the color
In the centre of the sun,
Which flared outward
In the shape of a flower.
The arising to Heaven of an Angel, in cobalt fire,
Brings Sacredness.
Which is the colour of abstraction,
An abstract ascension.
The cobalt fire mixed with blue,
Is an incense of Love
That cradles innocence and power
In the way that Christ embraces
The child,
The child who is born as a star,
A star born of light
Who seeks the light
And in a vehemence known to the light
Rises up to the light
Through devotion and reverence
To that which is termed the Father,
And the Father which resides in the heart.

Morgan Bobbie St. Claire

TO A WOMAN CALLED TIFFANY, A POEM

You splash in the centre of the sun
And find it brilliant!
You will even touch the wings of a bluebird
To feel its gentleness of hue.
(Remember, whenever you see bluebirds, think of Miriam.)
Or touch the wing of a falcon in flight
To feel its color of zeal.
The moon finds you beholden to
The gentle color of the Son —
The color of the Son being gold,
Which surges through rainbows
To become a powerful aureole
That flashes in the Earth
When it is dry.
Only to rise up again to grace the Sun
Which becomes silvery in its allure
And pure Gold in its Sweetness.
May the allure of the Moon
And the grace of the Sun
Always find you walking on enchanted ground.

TO A MAN CALLED ALEX, A POEM

Overtures of orchestrated magnificence
Touched with the obedience and love
Of a priest holding in his arms
A faded Bible that has
Golden jeweled brilliance flaring from
The pages.
The music is rich and rare
And resides in the Bible as words
Which are beatified through the
Love of the Father.
And remember
The dogwood, which is beatified
As the master Jesus is beautiful.
And those humble flowers are known to be
On the wings of a dove, as the Lord
Has the Holy Spirit descend upon him
In Holy Vibration to say,
"This is my beloved Son."

Morgan Bobbie St. Claire

Starkeepers

Starkeeper of the sun and Starkeeper of the Earth, you are beautiful Light Beings who spin your knowledge through the Universal Man and Universal Woman, drawing up through the outside of a real world to a spiritual world, whirling outwards to mystical worlds, and greeting throughout the beautiful Cosmos the beautified Rose.

Golden visions touch my soul and erupt through my psyche as a fountain of emotion that I cannot contain.

Prayer without ceasing leads me to the foot of the cross, wherein lies my salvation. Our hope, to encounter a resurrection of the soul; our inspiration, to give us steps on Earth for the liberation of the spirit. And, finally, the release of old energies and the birth of a reality that "is not of this world," so completely that the real world fades and another world develops that is the golden transport of everlasting life. When the soul, once liberated, can travel to a dimension, or Heaven, which is so sweet—a man or a woman can truly say, "I love."

Jesus, Beauty of Eternity, stamp upon my soul the beauty of thy features and let the words from thy grace so adorn my spirit that my recitation of words will be pronounced with joy, so much so that I will say, "Abba, let Thy will be done, not mine."

By the tears that fall without stopping from my eyes, may the Light of Saint Mary show me the reason for my tears, and then through the grace of Mary, when the reason for my tears are known, may I weep again.

TO ARTTAMUS, A POEM

Through the looking glass
That become, somehow, stained glass,
You look in
And see an Angel
Wearing the colors of the Bible.
Walking strong,
You walk through realities
That are paved with
The colors of the Son.
And the windows flare
As a ray from the Sun
Finds itself touching,
Grace upon grace,
The Golden Crown of Saint Mary
Of the House of the Father.
Yourself, Arttamus,
With hands that have touched roses,
You touch the stained glass.
Look in,
And then you are looking at an Angel.

A CHRISTMAS STORY

Angel Gabriel makes his way
With golden wing to golden heart
With words as sweet as these:
"Sweet Mary birthed a child
Two thousand years ago.
Hail, full of grace."
Joseph, the clement child's
Virginal adoptive father
Was called to the Temple of Jerusalem
Because he was begat to the house of David.
Mary was fourteen,
And,
The Holy Spirit had descended
Upon the rod, or staff, of Joseph
From whence a flower bloomed,
Then Mary and Joseph were betrothed and wed.
There was a star that came out of Jacob
With a sceptre emerging from Israel.
The child was born in a manger in Bethlehem,
Or perhaps a cave.
And the three Magi, who were known as
Gaspar, Melchoir, and Balthasar,
Who had travelled 900 miles from Persia,
Gathered around the little Messiah
Who was surrounded by light
As bright as the sun.
So! Come all ye faithful
To the Temple of Jerusalem
To see the holy Lord child

Given the name Jesus from Emmanuel
And blessed in that Temple
By Simeon and Anna.
Anna being a prophetess of age
Who found the shadow of a cross upon his brow.
It had been a long journey
For Joseph and Mary to Bethlehem
From Nazareth through the mountains of Cana
For the census decreed by Caesar Augustus.
Eighty miles they had both travelled
By foot and by colt, in three days' time.
The Magi left gifts that were essential:
Of gold, myrrh, and frankincense.
And, not long after Jesus' birth
Came the flight into Egypt.
A sorrow of Mary;
But maybe the child Jesus,
The Prince of Peace,
Began His learning of
"I and the Father are one," whence in Egypt.

THE BLESSED VIRGIN

Thy eyes are as blue as forget-me-nots.
Wild lilies in your arms.
You have white flowers upon your very yellow shoes.
White flowers of light.
You wear six rings of diamonds.
These diamonds are from the sun
Or have drifted on stars.
What flows through those diamonds
Is light from thy precious soul,
And that light is powerful.
When a grace is asked for and not forgotten
Your gems glow with the fire of white sapphires.
When a grace to be asked for is forgotten,
Those diamonds emit the light of sadness.
However, that light is always,
World without end,
Vehement and loving and powerful.
The Blessed Virgin, with her power
Can cause the sun to fall from the sky.
"Hail Mary, full of grace."
And as the sun is falling from the sky
It almost touches the Earth in its great energy,
While at the same time
Mary gives the golden globe of Earth
To Heaven.

Roses and countless other flowers,
Our Lady's tears to Mary's Glory,
From wearing a veil for Golden Jerusalem,
To the lowering of a veil
From those of her children who wear a veil
So they may carry flowers.
Saint Mary is so beautiful
That she will always be called Beautiful
And totally Radiant.

THE SCEPTER OF QUEEN MARY

At the edge of the rainbow —
At the edge of time —
The magnificent King stood tall and golden
In the colors of the Son.
He stood in the song of Heaven
And he held in his hand a gold rose.
The gold rose was a scepter
Of the Queen of Heaven
And the jewels of the scepter
Were a secret to the crown,
While the woman of the Crown
Wore the colors of the Sun:
White, yellow, blue, and purple.
Sapphires, rubies, emeralds, and pearls
Cover the Throne of Messiah.
The Throne of the woman of the Immaculate Heart
Is made of secret gems
That cause Angels to weep.
Queen Mary's words are the gentlest on Earth,
Yet with the strongest will
She is Incarnate Grace and Wisdom born.
Hail! Holy Queen!
As she wraps her arms around each beautiful child of God.

THE STARS OF MARIGOLD

The Son mixed with Gold
Finds the Sun in the sky
To be rapt in its beauty.
With marigolds sweet,
Resting poignantly
In the hand of Mary's Son.
(Marigolds symbolize Mary's simplicity and sorrow.)
As the sun glances from her diamond
Which is made of Light
And is spun from bright gold
That pierces the night
While stars in the sky
Are born as children.
The children reach for the stars,
Of which there are twelve,
And, as they seek to emulate
The perfection of Mary,
They touch each star,
With the light from each star
Passing through the virtue
Of the twelve attributes of Mary.
The twelve attributes of Mary
Flow from her Crown
Of secrets
And flow with love
To the heart of each child
She loves.

BRIDE OF THE CHURCH

Queen Mary, Bride of the Church,
And of the Immaculate Conception,
Radiates the beauty of the rose.
The rose was born in the heart of Mary,
Which spoke of her sinlessness and purity,
Sweetness and shyness.
The flowers of the Grace of the Father,
Touched her hair:
Daffodils, which are Mary's Crown,
And a flower known as Dianthus Caryophyllus,
Which is Mary's Love of God.
The flowers of the Grace of the Son
Touched her hands and feet:
Crown Daisy and Capers Bushes,
Shown on the Shroud of Turin.
And the children bore crocuses,
A penitent's rose,
In their beautiful hands
As they sang songs to Heaven
To the Bride of the Church and Mother of Christ.
While Angel's tears touched rose petals,
Which fell with love and sorrow
To touch the hand of God,
And to touch the hand of His children
While they carried lilacs and geraniums
For Our Lady Beautiful
To the Highest Altar.

Morgan Bobbie St. Claire

ARMOR OF LIGHT FOR THE SACRED HEART

An ancient star sang out
Hallelujah to the Heavens
As the people rejoiced in miracles.
The lame did walk,
The blind did see,
And the water poured
As the rain poured.
The words of the Lord
Poured forth as well.
And then there came a day
When the Apostles wept
Because it was the day
When the Lord wore his armor of Light.
Bitter fell the tears
As the mighty truth of Jesus
Rested against the sky.
Then the rain fell; in darkness was the sky.
And then
The Golden God called Man-Transformed
Ascended unto Heaven.
The bitter tears
Had touched the hand of God.
Touched, too, the Ocean of Mercy,
And the water and the Blood
Had become
The Sacred Heart of Jesus.
Thus, from the New Adam

Came a Golden Heart
That had been pierced
And a crown of thorns,
Which represents Jesus' suffering for man.
Drops of Blood fell from the Sacred Heart of Jesus,
And as they fell
So did His tears.
And a new garden was thus made
Called the Garden of Heaven.

THE SORROWFUL

I am so very tender in my own sacredness
To offer you a petal of a very real rose.
The real rose is yellow, the color of joy.
And as I offer you joy,
I think upon *Mata Dolorosa*,
The Sorrowful Mother,
Saying to her children of the Rosary,
"Through penitence comes forgiveness
And the 'saving' of a broken heart."
The mountains wept in Jerusalem
Where Jesus walked His last evening.
"I was there. And I saw hosannas
As He sat upon a snow white colt.
Then I saw the Chalice,
And as the wine became clear with Light,
I sipped its nectar."
Then Jesus left the table of plenty.
There were tears streaming from His face.
He prayed in the vast mountains of Jerusalem,
Mountains that wept.
And our Lord became anointed again
Through the weeping of the mountains.
There was perfume that filled the air
Before He departed,
And He was anointed again by a woman's tears.
The sun had set

And all the Father had to do was
Make a miracle in the sky:
A miracle to save the Savior.
But the Savior was God born
So the God-Man said nothing, but
"If you will but take this cup from me!"
And the Sun (who is the Father)
Brilliant in Light of all kinds, said
"Thou are my Beloved Son. "
And so another teardrop fell
That caused grief more than any could know
For our Sorrowful Mother, Mary.
And the children of the Rose
Are sorrowful, too.
We love the Christ:
Crucified, resurrected, ascended to Heaven.
And we adore the Rose.

THE COLORS OF THE SKY

The color of the Son
Was golden on the wing
Of a bird who was a sparrow.
The color of the Son
Was immaculate as well,
As were the colors of the Sun.
The colors of the Son
Flared like colors of the rainbow,
And these colors went right to
Our Lady of Golden Israel.
The colors of the Son
Were mainly red and yellow:
Red for a cloak and yellow for the Sun.
And for Our Lady the colors were
The hue of every rose.
And the colors of the Son
Flowed through the colors of the roses
Like a Rosary that is held
When carrying crocuses.
A sweet flower of penitence
Whose scent was also sweet
As the devotion of the Fragrance of the Father.
And to the devotion of the Flower of Jerusalem.

FLOWERS OF THE SUN

May the glory of Saint Mary
Echo 'round the Lamb of the Golden Stars,
And may the fragrance of the glory
Seek penitence in flowers.
Reparation is the flower
To the rising of the Son.
And the flowers of the Sun
Were Edelweiss (Purity of Mary)
And Pentitent's Rose,
Which shone with adoration of the hour.
And Geraniums and the Iris
Recited a song to Our Lady
With the passion of the rain
Through the rainbow of the Sun.
And the children of the Son
Wept for adoration of the Assumption
With Larkspur and Ivy being where Mary
And where God has walked, too.
And the Madonna Lily gracefully adorns my door to Heaven:
The symbol of the Glory of Saint Mary's Heart.
And I listen to Her voice
That is the voice of many spring waters
For conversion and redemption
From the Power of the Throne.

Saint Mary intercedes for us
In the secret of the hour,
And the Angel of Gentleness says,
"Say a prayer of lamentation to God,
For through thy lamentation comes
The satiation of thy sorrowful soul
From the Mercy of the Crown."

THE MESTICA MADONNA

The Beautiful Mother of God
Knew a child in Guadalupe
With pungent Castilian flowers
Held lovingly in his hands.
The Aztec Temple of Tanantzin
Was divine
And known as Mother Earth,
Or,
As Mother Mary
To the children of Mexico.
The beautiful Cathedral
In divine Mexico
Has the precious children of the Rose,
Like Juan Diego,
In blissful and penitent prayer
As they
"Fall on their knees"
To bless the Blessed Virgin Queen.
And the Castilian roses
Transformed into the form of a Cross
After the Image of the Virgin
Was imprinted on the flowers.
And the children
And the mothers and fathers of Guadalupe
Carry flowers in their arms:
A symbol of the Mystical Rose.

DAUGHTER OF JERUSALEM

O Light of Nazareth
Queen of the Rosary
With beauty of shyness.
Secrets of hidden mystery
Have unfolded in you
Thousands of times.
Flowers from the well of God
Embrace you, Mary.
And precious zephyrs carried you
When you assumpted to Heaven.
Your mouth is as sweet
As the red roses of Jacob,
Whose name was Israel.
And thou art the Daughter of Jerusalem.
(The city called Jerusalem is the daughter of Israel.)
Thy beautiful blue eyes are the color of sapphires
That weep in the Sun.
And thy beautiful children of Adam
Adore thee.

SWEET ROSE OF SHARON

As the sweet rose of Sharon (a rosary)
Was held in hand by One
Whose voice echoed passion
Throughout a land of grace,
The very mountains wept
To hear His name on Earth.
And Heaven pronounced him King
As Earth pronounced His name
As Emmanuel,
"God with us,"
And also Prince of Peace.
The sweet rose of Sharon
Shed petals of Light
That cascaded through the Heavens
On a rosary divine.
And as the petals drifted
From Sweet Mary to her Son,
He said, "Hail Mary, Queen of Sharon,
I'll give you a rose for thy delight."

THE VINEYARDS

The very trees of Jerusalem
Were strong and beautiful and sweet.
As the Lord Jesus walked through
These vineyards
He said, "Each vineyard must be perfect,
And if there is a tree
That lacks in strength and beauty sweet,
I'll hold it in my arms
Like a child of Israel
Until the leaves begin to shine."
And the Light of the Radiant Lamb
Found teardrops on the leaves
As the beauteous trees of sorrow
Sought forgiveness from the Lamb.
And the Lamb of Gold said,
"My children of sorrow,
Come to Me, all you that labor,
And are burdened, and I will refresh you.
And also say a rosary
For Our Lady of Sorrow,
The very Rose of Heaven.
And as you say a rosary,
Say also to the Lord,
'The love of the Lamb has made me perfect,
And I'll be in Heaven with Jesus and Mary one day.'"

THE JEWEL OF SIMON PETER

The wondrous Sea of Galilee
(Beauteous sapphire jewel)
Accepts upon its mysterious waters
The figure of the Master Jesus
Walking with such love
And with such faith.
Jesus said to Simon Peter,
"Have faith, Peter,
Like a child,
And walk with me on the jewel,
The powerful sea of Galilee."
And Peter took faith,
And could not fall,
And the jewel shone with Light
As the song of Saint Peter
Rose in melody
And, grace upon grace, a blessing was wrought
On that jewel, called then, Galilee.

THE TRANSFIGURATION

Along the slopes of Mount Tabor
There was an illumination
That was the transfiguration
Of the Master Jesus.
There was the Presence
Of a white light
That descended from His Father in Heaven
That covered the beauteous features
Of this God-Man.
As the precious white light
Consumed His very being
He was beatified through
The intense Vibration of God
And thus,
Converted and Man-Transformed
He became "a light unto the world."

GOLDENNESS OF HEAVEN

The passion of the Virgin
Placed roses in my soul
And the pungent scent was vivid
As it spun to Light from Gold.
The air was delicate
As bluebirds soared and drifted
Around the Angels of Heaven.
And the Goldenness of Heaven
Became saturated with petals
Of dogwood.
The dogwood was white
And virginal
And the scent it left in sorrow,
And the sweet cloak of the Master Jesus
Was as beatified as dogwood flowers.

THE POWER OF THE LAMB

A sigh swept throughout Jerusalem
And the Golden Temple (which is Jesus) stood
Amidst a crown of thorns and sorrow.
God-Man, who is the Master Jesus—
The mortal face of God, and the
Sacred countenance of man—
Was crucified.
And as His radiance ascended to Heaven.
There was a cloak surrounded by
Bluebirds and the gold of the sun,
Worn by a woman,
Mother of the eternal Word made flesh,
And she ascended to Heaven as well,
Body and soul:
Our Lady, who was born without original sin.
Jesus suffered through an ocean of bitterness
Only to touch Divine waters
That were the Ocean of Mercy.
And Sweet Mary suffered seven sorrows
From whence bloomed the Roses of her
Very Immaculate Heart,
Immaculate Roses of forgiveness.
Throughout the ascension,
And even before the ascension,
Was the Power and the Love
Of the Lamb
Who was glorified.
And His children of Radiance
Are glorified through the love of the Lamb.

THE GOLDEN RAIN

The fever of the Sun
Left me breathless
As I knelt in prayer
Humbly,
Before the Master
Of the Golden Sun.
His name is Infinite Majesty,
The Tabernacle of the Most High.
Also, Desire of the Everlasting Hills,
And, Patient and Most Merciful.
He has walked with all of us,
He has heard each sparrow sing.
He has touched each child's tear.
"Children of Radiance, come unto me
All heavily laden,"
He has uttered with love,
Like a rare jewel of beauty
Glistening on the edge of yesterday.
With passion emitting from each heart
As we touch the hand of Jesus
Or, even so, have touched
A tear on petals of roses.
"Hail, Holy Queen. Let us pray
As we seek reconciliation with God."
The Golden Rain that falls
From the skies
Is Radiance
That blesses field and flower——
Fields that we have ran in

And flowers we have given with devotion
To bring about love,
With flowers as a way
Of obtaining grace
For sanctification.
"Lady Ephesus, I weep in my soul
Whenever I behold thy blessedness.
My God! How I love thee!"

A MAGI

There stood a man
Atop a hill,
A hill near the Valley of Snow.
And an Angel stood
At the foot of the hill
Who said to the man,
"Look!
In the sky!
Look at the Star of Gold.
That is a Star from Heaven.
Follow the light to a stable
Where a clement child will be born
Whose name will be Emmanuel."
The man was a Magi
Who left his hill.
He saw the splendor of the Angel
He heard the message of his words,
And he decided he would speak to the shepherds
When he reached the Valley of Snow
(Which is termed Bethlehem).
After the Angel stopped speaking
The Magi began to weep
Because a prophecy had been given
About a Messiah
Who would be born in light,
And who would teach the people
How to be of peace and joy
Through becoming at one with the Father.
And then, one day

The ocean of love
Became bitter.
The Messiah was crucified-—
But he in His Eternal Beauty
Ascended
Unto the very Gates of Heaven,
Where he is enthroned as Messiah.
But the Magi wept because the child Clement
Was the Lord.

RELEVANCY TO DIVINITY

The feeling of relevancy to divinity
And of love that is important
Comes from a heart that knows sorrow
And from a heart that knows love.
Through the Sacred Heart of Jesus,
Who has known great sorrow and deep pain,
Came love rushing outward
From an Ocean of Mercy
Like a fountain of beauty.
Through our divinity we are
Culled and selected
By the Holy Host,
By the One God called the Holy Trinity.
Our divinity through our understanding
Of lifetimes
Bequeaths to us our love
And our devotion to the One God.
Devotion to God is to be so complete
That the individual says
"Abba, thy will be done."

In the hands of God
Rests my valor and my heroism,
My love and my truth,
And the absolute beauty of my soul.

The sparrow flies,
But takes shelter while a falcon
Flies with zeal and with passion,
With vision and with voice
Through the skies touched with rose.
"I am an Eternal Daughter of the Father.
I walk tall,
Carrying roses and crystals,
And I look at the Father
With love and utter devotion, and I say,
'I give my thanks to you, Father,
For you are good
And your mercy endures forever.
I was born in Thy House
And Thy goodness and mercy
Shall follow me all the days of my life.'"

JEWEL OF THE SUN, JEWEL OF THE FATHER

There was a jewel of the Father
Who was born of the Silver Moon,
His name was Clement.
One day, as he was walking
Through the Judean Desert
Toward the mountains of Israel,
He saw a bluebird.
He said to his mother, Miriam,
"Look! There! Whenever I see bluebirds
I'll think of you, Sweet Miriam,
Jewel of the Sun."
Then there was the Light
From the Golden Star
That had passed to the Silver Moon.
That fiery Golden Star
Had touched somehow the Light
Of the very beauteous Father
And had become as gentle
As the Light of the Silver Moon.
And Miriam said, "Whenever I see the Golden Star,
Or the Silver Moon,
I'll think of you, my Son,
Jewel of the Father."

PROPHET OF THE GOLDEN SUN

The honey lay in a field
Where it enfolded the Star Sun,
Then the honey fell with ease
To the Prophet of the land.
The Prophet lifted up his pure hands
To the Golden Sun, and said,
"The honey drifted in a flower of the sun,
And when it drifted
The honey dreamed a dream with the Sun.
The dream with the Sun
Was a whisper to the Father."
And the dream was about a Prophet
Who lifted up his pure hands to the Golden Sun
So the Prophet could say:
"Morning and evening prayers
Look like diamonds and sapphires
Glistening in the Sun."
The Son of God enfolds them like wild honey
In the flowers of the morning,
And in the evening
The Prophet of Grace holds a cup
Called a Holy Chalice
Made of sapphires and diamonds from Heaven
From which there is honey and wine.

THE STORY OF MOSES

You are a wanderer
Just like Saint Issa,
And you have jewels to give away
As you talk about God appearing
In the desert
When there was a storm
At the night time.
A storm that calmed a Burning Bush
Before God, the God of Heaven,
Found out the Bush was burning.
Yet the Burning Bush drew a sigh
Of expectancy and beauty
For those who were watching.
And the allure of the Maiden
Of the Rose of Sharon
Before such a secret was known
Blessed the Gold Fire
That was not cold or hot,
And then she wept tears
Because she could not speak.
The night is not long
But where there is weeping
Where secrets are born
There is Silver Music
And writing in Light.
The writing was in Light
Because the Lord cared
And the Burning Bush
Would simply change form

To become a book of Light
That left tears of glory
And honor
For generations.
And the Maiden
Who was in the Desert of Sharon
Had adornments of roses in her hair
(Hail Mary, full of grace)
That were sighing.
Roses met with the past,
The heavy fragrance of flowers —
The same in the Desert of Sharon.

MYSTERY IN LIGHT

Mystery in Light
Made of gems
On the Holy Chalice
Of the Anointed, named Christos.
Hosannas were heard
Throughout Jerusalem
For the Beloved
Who was the Son,
And in its hearing there was joy
That touched the soul
Of Abraham when he was born.
Then there was the mystery
Of the Cross
Which carried with it
The forgiveness of Christos
And of all the saints and Apostles
In Heaven.
And where there was forgiveness,
There bloomed roses.
An Ave was heard by an Angel
That trembled on the edge of the Universe
And as it trembled
It became a sacred Song
That echoed throughout the Cosmos

As a "Hail Mary," a hymn of devotion
And rejoicing
That said, "Holy Woman of the Sun:
A tendril, a tear
Was put there by God
Because you are born of the Sun."
Divine Mercy, descending to Earth
In the Person of Virtue.

Fount gushing forth from the mystery
Of the most serene Trinity!
May a rosary be recited
For the love and devotion of the Adored.

A BIRTH

The cry from the desert
Can be heard
By the precious Blossom of Israel.
The cry from the desert
Was the first breath
That left my lungs
After a birth that left gratitude
And love from a mother
Because the mother had been kind
Who birthed the infant.
This woman was remembered
As the woman who did not forget
What Fragrance meant
To the Mirror of Justice: Saint Mary.
AUM was the first word I uttered
As India of Saint Issa sought me out.
Also, a blossom of romance
Of the Arjuna
Who touched the flower
Of my soul
And radiance issued forth
From each corolla.
So, now I wear a crown of Goldenness
That had touched pain
And gushed with rivers of sorrow.

But the pain and the sorrow
Touched the Merciful Shield of the Lord,
And, today, like a lion of gold,
I wear pure and luminous
Flowers in my hair.

QUEEN MARY, PROPHET OF JESUS

In the quiet of the morning hour
I sense a silence that is made of roses,
And the roses are likened to silken clouds
That impart a flushed hue of innocence
Upon a sky laden with rapture.
The rapture of the brilliant sky
Was known and felt by the Angels of God,
And the Angels touched each mysterious cloud
And then, a beautiful rose was gifted
To each rapturous cloud in the sky.
The Angels said, "Hail Mary, full of grace."
Saint Mary touched a rose
And sent a petal to God,
And God said, "Hail Mary, full of grace."
Sweet Mary began to weep
When she heard these words from the sky,
And the wetness of a single tear
Fell upon the robes of her Son.
"Hail Mary, full of grace," He said.
And Sweet Mary said,
"The grace was mine when you were conceived,
The grace was yours when you were born-
The grace of the Father has found me worthy,
And the grace of God follows thee."
The flowers of roses began to bloom
Like a river of rain
And a valley of sorrow.

Then, a mystery of joy and a mystery of glory
Took shape in the clouds
That surrounded the Earth.
The people wept, then the people rejoiced
Because, "Hail Mary, full of grace."
Queen Mary, Prophet of Jesus,
The perfume of roses
Touches the Earth and they say with grace,
"Hail Mary," graces all.

THE TWELVE ATTRIBUTES OF MARY

The white lily of the Virgin Queen
Was atop a hill,
A hill near the Moon and the Sun.
The White Lily was powerful and pure,
And was the purity of Love.
Atop that perfect hill
Stood Sweet Mary.
There were golden roses
That fell from her hands,
Which symbolized the beauty
Of the spirit of penitence.
And she walked like a goddess
Amidst English Daisies
Her flower of God (who is Jesus).
The tulip sprang from wherever she walked,
And the tulip is the Prayer of Mary.
And apple blossoms are the Crown of Mary,
World without end.
Twelve attributes of spirit, and Mary:
Charity, Joy, Peace,
Patience, Forbearance, Goodness,
Benignity, Mildness, Fidelity,
Modesty, Continency, Chastity.

Morgan Bobbie St. Claire

ROSES AND LIGHT

The sky was flushed with roses
And the air was keen and sharp.
There were birds of every description
That flew with the wind to God.
As the roses touched each bird's wing
There emitted a Song of Joy,
And the song was
The Song of the Rosary,
"Hail Mary, full of grace."
The sky was flushed with Light
That was radiant and sweet
As the Light touched each bird's wing —
The Light was of the Christ.

LOVE ONE ANOTHER

The birds are lightly flying
Through the dust and through the rain.
There's a feeling on the threshold
Of a rich effulgent desire
To meet the Gold in Heaven,
And for the Gold to meet
This saying from the Bible:
"Owe no man anything
Except to love one another
For he who loves his neighbor
Has fulfilled the Law."
And as the Sun ariseth in the sky
This saying fell as showers
Where the timeless birds flew.
And as each wing of bird
Flew through rain and dust,
There came Goldenness from the Son
That sealed the feeling with total trust.
The dust is from the desert
Where the Master Jesus walked in the Sun,
And the rain falls from the hands and feet
Of the Radiance called the Son.

The heavenly rain that fell in Jerusalem
Was as golden as each bird's wing
That sought, with flight together with the wind,
The trust that is complete:
"Owe no man anything
Except to love one another
For he who loves his neighbor
Has fulfilled the Law."
Amen.

MORNING RISING

In the days of this life
I have known weeping and affliction
Through the Sorrowful Immaculate Heart of Mary
And through the Sorrowful Sacred Heart of Jesus.
May I confess of my sin to thy perfect ear
Savior Sweet of the world,
Bright Light of our luminous texture of thought.
The powerful cross of Jerusalem
Speaks my pardon.
Through my reconciliation with God
And through the virtue of His holy wounds
I come to kneel humbly before my Lord.
Beauteous Fountain of all holiness
In anticipation of forgiveness
From thy Divine Heart of Mercy.
The White Lily of the Trinity watches us
As a Mother and as our Queen.
And, as Woman Transformed
Who cometh forth as the morning rising.
And through the rising of the morning
Comes a shining day of glory
Through the love of Mary and through the glory of the Lamb.

Morgan Bobbie St. Claire

ZARA OF THAMAR

There rested on the edge
Of the prophet's words
Fire from ancient knowledge.
The fire
Was an opal that was spun from golden light.
And the prophet's words
Were words of justice
And words of prophecy.
He said, "I AM Zara of Thamar,
A man from the Tribe of Israel.
There will be born to the
House of Abraham
A child,
And his name shall be called Clement.
He will speak words of
Faith, love, and charity.
And His words will be fiery, yet sweet,
As a bird on the edge of the wind
Winging his way back to God
With the songs God taught him to sing."
The syllables that Zara spoke
Were of rhapsody and beauty
And they spilled through the air
As prophecy
Before Jesus was born.
"A King, a Man of silence and of
Spoken words that will be sanctified.
Wherefore,

He will be crucified
At the Valley of the Son (which is Calvary)
For the sins of His people,
And then
On the third day
He will be called
The Arisen Christ.

THE WHITE ROSE OF SHARON

The white rose of Sharon
Was known in Egypt 3,000 years ago.
It was brought to Egypt by an Angel
Who prophesied the birth of Queen Mary.
In his prophesy, he included
The birth of Saint Mary.
Joachim and Saint Anne were told
Mary would be born as the result of an oath.
She was presented to the Temple of Jerusalem
When an infant,
And did not leave the Temple until she was
Twelve years old.
Saint Mary was given a white lily
By an Angel, then by her chosen husband.
And when Joseph and Mary and their son
Fled to Egypt,
Mary was given an Eternal White Rose of Sharon,
Because Sharon did mean
Baptism of the betrothed.
Wed to the Holy Spirit was she
In all her humbleness.
Egypt was important to Mary and Jesus,
And Joseph, too,
Because of the laws of nature
And the laws of God
Written in such a fashion that Jesus could truly say,
"The Father and I are one."

THE SONG OF THE ROSARY

Rushing like a fountain
Of great beauty
There was the sound
Of the song of the Rosary.
And from the sound
Of the Song of the Rosary
Issued forth a psalm of joy
Like the baptism of a minister.
Their arose high within the mountains
The sound of Golden music
That told each heart to be still.
The desire of the Everlasting Mountains
Was felt from each peak, with grace
And felt atop each pinnacle
That said, "I am the Beloved Master,
My name is Desire of the Everlasting Mountains.
I have a Sacred Heart, abode of justice and love,
And full of goodness—follow me."
May prayer, adoration, and reverence be sent like a dove
To the heart of Jesus
To be blessed by the Most Holy Sacrament.

A STAR BORN

A beauteous star
Drifts from on high
And falls from the sky
When a child is born
Complete in his or her completeness.
He or she is everything to the Father.
The star became the child,
Born,
And the child
Radiates
His or her perfection
Through the expanding
Lotus of the soul.
And through the expanding
Lotus of the soul,
Comes the knowledge and the completion of a circle
A Circle within the Sun.

A PANTHER ACKNOWLEDGES GRACE

Children walk with God in their souls,
And their innocence touches
With simplicity and devotion
The mountains where Jesus walked
When he was in prayer to God.
Yellow flowers are garlands of love
That touch the forehead of the beautiful children,
And these wreathes of grace
Speak of the circle of the Sun
Where the panther acknowledges a grace so divine
That tears fall from his eyes
In a feeling of such profound gratitude and elegance
That the circle of the Sun touches the clouds of eternity,
Where some may see God,
And others will weep without stopping,
And others will touch the Sun that is the Son
And say, "May the circle remain unbroken."

THE PRAYER BEADS

The rosary vibrates at a speed
That, in the Temple of Grace,
Is so remarkable
It brings tears to the face of Christ.
The vibration is a whisper
To the lovingness of God
Who is termed the Father,
And the whisper is a prayer
That entwines itself around
The prayer beads
Of the Immaculate Conception.
The count of man is infinity
As God's eye rests upon the sparrow,
And the count of Christ is endless
In a world that holds no turmoil.
But sorrow can reside
Upon the restless ocean that is smooth,
Which riots with pure wisdom, reason, and love,
And the perfume of the very rich wind
That speaks of bliss and romance;
The romance of the Christ.
"Peace on Earth to men of good will!"
Are words uttered in Gold,
And on Earth as it is in Heaven.
And Goldenness the Christ shall bring
To every peaceful man.

IN THE UNKNOWN GROTTO

I felt today a child's touch of grace
And in her hands were lovely roses.
Our Lady was saying a prayer
In a grotto that was unknown.
As the flowers left the child's lovely hands,
Petals fell to the ground in the grotto,
And the child said, "Hail Mary, full of grace."
The Virgin Mary said,
"My Son, Jesus, full of immaculate Grace,
Was at your side when you were born.
Do you feel the grief of my Son
When seven sorrows touched my heart?
And the crown that Jesus wore
Was a crown of mine as well,
A mortal crown of thorns
That touched my own forehead, too."
The child began to weep
And her tears were tears of such pain.
The tears fell in the grotto,
And then roses began to bloom.

THE GOLDEN STEEPLE

The Golden Steeple
That bore a Cross
Was loved by untold thousands.
Its shadow of Gold
Against the sky
Promised redemption and love
To the sacred
And to the children
Of the Light.
And the glow of Love
And Peace
Touched each beloved soul
With such serenity and grace
That Saint Mary in Heaven,
Singular Vessel of Devotion,
Bestowed petals of grace and beauty
To her beautiful children of the Rose.

SAINT ISSA AS A PROPHET OF LIGHT

Earth Star and Sun Star give their light
To a flowing love that cascades
Through the meadowlands in a dance
That is a festivity of the children.
Through the festivity poured the wine of the Master,
Saint Issa.
And through the light of the children
Issued manna from Heaven
That was desirable because it was good.
The Holy Grail moved like a dove
At the Feast of the Ancients.
And as the Holy Grail moved
Amidst light passing through the gems and the wine,
There came forth the eyes of the seeing
From the eyes of the blind.
Saint Issa travelled as a Prophet of Gold:
Born in the light,
Lived in the light,
Loved the light,
And taught in the light.
His words were written in light,
And uttered in Gold.
In the time of Saint Issa
There was a vibrancy that rushed like a river
Throughout all of Nazareth,
As well as Persia, India, Tibet.
That vibrancy trembled like a tear:
Then the tear fell
And the sorrow was unbearable.

But the Beauteous Eternal Father
Caused the Beautiful to ascend,
And through Saint Issa's ascension
Came the grace, the blessing, and the adoration
Of the sacred.
"Hail Mary, full of grace."
Born without original sin
The mother of God, did too,
Have from wine and gems light that was the Nectar
Of Christ Consciousness.

THE HEAVENS OPEN LIKE A FLOWER

The Heavens open to reveal
The roses
Of the Sweetness of the Eternal Rose,
Saint Mary.
Each rose is for a meditation
On the beauty of each person's life,
As it merges with the Holiness
Of the Sweet Rose of Heaven,
And with the Sacramental life
Of the Avatar Saint Issa, who is Jesus.
The Heavens open like a flower
For everyone of good will,
And the perfume of that flower
Rises all the way to Heaven
With joy to the Absolute,
And returns to Earth as an aroma so beautiful
It teaches with grace to each person.
Each person of good will is a god or a goddess
Born with the Gold of Divine Mercy
In their heart.
They are radiant, sweet, humble, and holy,
And love God...
So, that is all.

LORD, MAY I WALK WITH YOU?

God the Son,
House of God,
And Glory of the Radiance of Heaven,
Bless this house I live in
Which bears no marks on hands or feet
As yours did, dearest Savior.
And no marks from thorns upon my forehead,
Whilst yours was pierced so bitterly.
But, God-Man who dwells on High,
In the weeping of my soul,
I met your Passion on the way to Calvary
And I did say, "Lord, may I walk with you?"
You said, Lord: "Hold my hand while I walk
To Heaven with you."
By those words, I knew you loved me greatly,
And throughout that walk
You were quiet, Jesus.
You know, my spirit was truly wounded
By the scourging at the Pillar.
And I found no crown of thorns
Because I was not king
As you were, Lord, King of God's Kingdom
And King of Israel.
And I found the cross too heavy to bear,
But in my soul I embraced that cross
With tears of such gratitude.
And my hands and feet were pierced
Because yours were, Lord.
And throughout it all, Jesus,

Your goodness preserved me.
"My Shepherd, feed my soul
As I walk to Heaven with you."

Upon Leaving This Earth for Heaven

I rose as an Angel to Heaven, and as I rose up, my body lost most of its density. I rose up unencumbered to Heaven, with violet wings and I saw lambent waterfalls that cascaded with silver tones of music to rose and emerald and blue and mauve meadowlands of joy. The great sun in the sky did not give off heat, it was an orb of beauty that gave Light. And there were stars that knew no count.

The mountains of Heaven were amethyst and rose crystal, and from the summit of these mountains Angels resounded their sublime music. From the proud peaks of these mountains in Heaven there emitted a Gold Halo of magnificence, an Immortal Light that reflected the Holy Spirit.

The flowers of these mountains and in the meadowlands of Heaven were profuse, and there were birds in Heaven of scarlet, blue, and gold wing whose music as they sang became the music of God.

The sinew and vigor of my strength was perceived through the oceans of Heaven, peaceful motion that rhymed with power—an echo of my soul. I saw pure water all rainbow-hued become a blush of zeal that was serene and hushed yet rioted; where no restlessness was caused, but rather inspiration that was potent poetry emitting a radiance for this Angel with violet wings.

Weeping that existed as tears on Earth became tears of forgiveness in Heaven. The weeping brought exalted feelings of worth and comprehension without suffering in Heaven. Any pain I felt on Earth almost evaporated, not even resembling wisps of sorrow to burden my soul in Heaven.

The worlds I came across in Heaven were surreal, swirling with color and the poetry of absolute joy that was refreshing and pulsing with the merit of the truly great teachers: -Buddha, Jesus, Krishna, the Great Spirit, Paramahansa Yogananda, Saint Mary, Nithyananda Dhyanapeetam, Namah Sivaya, Muhammad, Brahman. Emotion and instruction exploded from these great teachers, and other great teachers. Parents, siblings, educators, healers, friends, priests, all those people who have been loved by me and who have loved me for how many past lifetimes as they prepared me for rebirth. Divinity was the expression of exaltation and ecstasy that was expressed in rapture in my soul as I sat at the holy feet of these great teachers, learning and setting a path of ancient astrology and celestial pathways of enlightenment.

Saint Mary in Heaven became the teacher of the Immaculate Conception; she wore robes of tender grace that were not blue anymore but became Gold to delineate the transfer of truth known through life on Earth. So beautiful in Heaven it resembled God.

Jesus in Heaven is the Temple who teaches thought processes that are vocal and of the Holy Vibration, and what He taught in Heaven is: "Behold the Son of Man will be seen ascending to Heaven with Angels ascending and descending around the Son of Man." Behold, the Son of Man was always the Son of God. The Angels of Heaven envelop Christ, who-said-"I AM," and the vibrational count of Christ is infinity.

In the centre of my forehead is the Christ-seeing and through that seeing is the Visionary who is chimerical, the mystic, with a reality so profound in a world of beauty that rhapsody has become my divine sentiment. As a Universal Woman, I can say: "I am the fragrance of the Earth, and as I leave this Earth for Heaven, I'll become the fragrance of Heaven."

THE FATHER RESIDES IN EACH HEART

The days are flaunting autumn leaves
And Autumn charm.
The stars of Heaven
Are born to God
As God's begotten children.
The Light from the central sun
Is radiating Christ,
And the very beautiful Father
Is saying,
"Sons and daughters of my own
You were begotten long ago
In my own image, like the Son."
And the Son sits
On the Throne of Messiah
Where the Angels of Messiah,
The Angels of Triumph,
Bear the conqueror's Cross
Because Jesus conquered death
And He conquered the world as well.
He is powerful, and called
Radiant and Beautiful
Throughout the Seasons of the Father.
And, too, the glorious Master
Laid His life down for His sheep.
As we are, too,
Lambs of Christ
Eternal children of Jesus.

Morgan Bobbie St. Claire

Remember, too, that friendship gained
Does not compulsion bear
But is born of love and mercy,
Joy and peace, and unconditional
It sets truly the pricelessness
Of treasures that are sweet.
"I and the Father are one,"
Jesus said.
And the gift of immortality
Belongs to all God's children.
And don't forget those
That seek or have found God.
God resides in your very heart:
Known as the Father.

PLACE OF THE GODS

There were spirals to the clouds,
And the spirals were hard to find,
And it was hard to climb to a place of Golden Temples
Where the gods resided.
The gods were gentle.
And every once in a while
A beautiful saint would find a way
To the spirals to the clouds,
Walk up the steps to the Golden Temples,
And the gods would say,
"We have books for you to read, Child,
Books that are old and have dust on them.
We also have jewels
That we will adorn you with
Before you leave. And we will, with love, tell you
About the jewels of Light you will be adorned with.
It could be the Buddha's medicine jewelry,
It could be a flute of Krishna,
It could be a staff of the Master Jesus,
It could be a crystal of Merlin of the round table,
Or a rosary of such unusual Light
That the stars in the sky would weep.
You may visit when you sleep,
And we, the gods, will be wakeful for your coming.
And if the spiral to the clouds
Is too hard to find, little sainted children,
We'll show you the way."

SRI ANANDAMAYI MA, SAINT OF INDIA

In the beauty of her countenance
I beheld a grace and purity
That had touched her soul
And shone through her eyes of radiance.
The Divinity of her form
Lent address to her teachings,
And her teachings were mystical and advanced
In the way of a self-realized saint of God.
"I am the same," she said.
Born, married, rising from this Earth to Heaven.
And "I am the same."
My soul is as it was in the Beginning,
As it is today at-one with God.
And "I am the same,"
As born in the image of God.
Her depth of the understanding of concepts
That are God-realized and mystical
Are profound in their musical sound
And Universal rhythm of poetry spoken through words
That were religious and humble,
And they touched the soul
With a deep stirring of memory.
This Mother of Permeated Joy
Is so divine in her countenance
That the children of God would touch her face
With tears of profuse love and joy.
And those tears once released
Would show flowers in the Earth how to be born.

THE REFLECTION OF THE MOUNTAINS

The Heart of the Father is adorned with flowers,
And the virtue of His Son is captured and reflected
In the many artists' pictures of the masters of paint.
Saint Mary is reflected in the Rosary,
And her own mother, Saint Anne, was rapturous
Upon the bearing of a child
Who was without original sin.
May you always see God through the reflected artwork
Of the many great masters.
And may the mountains that heave forth
Their innocence
Remind you of the Beatitudes
That were given by Jesus on Mount Kurun Hattin.
It was through the mountains that Jesus walked
When He prayed to the Father.
Thus, the mountains reflect the allure of the Master Jesus.
The Sun in the sky produces ecstasy
And rainbows of the Dragon are known to bless this Earth,
As the Lord of China blessed Jesus when he was in China.
Through the reflecting ecstasy of the Lord
May divinity and peace sanctify you
As a child of faith, hope, and charity.
And may the baptism of your heart
Radiate Love for always.

A PRAYER TO THE VIRGIN SAINT MARY

We are the adoration
And the cherished of the adored.
We are the adoration of Saint Mary,
Mother of Christ the Kind.
Through the prayer of the rosary
We come to kneel at the throne
Of the Rose of Nazareth, saying,
"Our Lady of Grace,
Divine Grace of God,
We seek refuge through thee to touch
The divine hand of your blessed Son
In contrition and love."
To touch, grace upon grace,
A sacred petal of the rose
Through the recitation of the rosary.
Through penitence, petition,
And through true sorrow and apology,
Which is felt at the hem of Saint Mary's blue cloak.
Saint Mary said, "I am the Dove of the Rose."
Salvation of the truly repentant can be found
Through the heavenly solace of the Divine Mother
Of our Lord.
And through the weeping of lament
Our sins may be washed away
And also through the grace of final perseverance.
Amen.

JERUSALEM FOUR-SQUARED

Fortune was at Jerusalem's gate
When the dragon moved his golden wings,
And through the whirring of gold
Brought ecstasy to the people
Of the Temple of the Sun.
In the Temple of the Son there was
Jerusalem four-squared..
And the twelve Tribes of Israel
Moved to the words of the priests
As they spoke words
That dwelt in the mountains and the deserts.
The fountains of grief and holy devotion
Rushed from emotion that did lament
And felt within the centre of the sun
The need of redemption,
Rooted in the soul,
And finally spilling outward
Like a dove enraptured.
The Apostles wore the armor
Of the God-Man of Israel
From whence flew the silent pain
Before they felt ecstasy
Through the resurrection of the Dove.

And the turning of the stone
Gave relief and forgiveness
To the children of Adam
From whence the gold of Jerusalem
Became the dragon
Who moved his golden wings
And brought ecstasy to the people
Of the Temple of the Sun.

PISCES, THE SIGN OF THE FISH

In the Meadowland (Jerusalem)
Of the Golden Lark (Jesus)
Stood a man who was
Peaceful and beautiful.
He had gold hair that was not short
And blue eyes that knew the tears
Of the Magnificent (the Apostles).
He had walked through the Valley of the Shadow
With the Master Jesus.
And, one day,
As he was walking through Galilee,
And then through a barren desert,
He suddenly knelt in a rapture of Light
After hearing a loud voice,
And drew in the sand a Fish.
The Angels of Jesus heard the sound of living waters
At the time that was Golden,
And they said, "Blessed be this man,
For he has put the Holy Grail
In the Sign of the Fish.
And it will be called in secret
The Sign of the Master, Pisces
And the man with gold hair will be called holy.

ETERNITY WRITTEN IN THE WIND

The cross of Saint Peter,
Appearing as flowers of fire
From the shrine of the Rider of the sun,
Saint Jerome,
Were worked into the four corners
Of the world.
From the four corners of the world
There were four chariots and horses,
And there was music that exploded
From the realms.
Walking through streets laden with roses,
And laden with the tears of the
Children of Light of the New World,
The music was perceived as a new direction
In which the sign of Saint Peter's cross
Was seen and given to the Children of the Light.
And a lily from Saint Joseph
Had been given in the desert
And the Children of the Light
Were transformed by the music of the realms.
Saint Jerome was like a preacher
Who rode on the wind
From the Sea of Galilee
To the four corners of the Earth
Where the Angel stood and said,
"Man of God and Prophet of the Storm,
You ride the wind like the child
Of the Holy Grail,

Who seeks Heaven through the divinity of your soul.
Stand in the sand of Eternity
And look into the eyes of the Master,
And you will see eternity
Written in the wind that says:
'I am the Dove of the Immaculate—
Look for me in the year of the Prophet
And you, Saint Jerome, will be reborn
Through the Power of the Lamb
And through the music of the son.'"

A Healing

In the presence of the Master Jesus there is a woman weeping a lament of sorrow for the child she loved who was ill. Her tears that fell from rain drops to God touched the hem of the Master's robes as He was walking to the market in Bethsaida and Jesus said, "The beautiful tears that have wet my cloak are tears that have set your child free." The woman said to the Master, "Touch in blessing the forehead of my son, if you will, so he will be made whole."

Jesus asked the child, who had eyes that the Father had made blue, to sit with Him for a moment. The child said, "My mother weeps for me, yet she has a rare disease herself, Rabbi." The Master smiled and the sun in the sky had trouble shining on the people in Bethsaida with its same brilliance.

"Diamonds and rust," said the Master. "Diamonds from the silver rain that weep for the child, and rust for the tears I'll weep for the woman."

SUNBURST

A sunburst of Light
Touches my soul
With grace and with song
As wings of gratitude and love
Sing to God of labor
Good and true.
The labor is of the staff
Of the Master Jesus.

FEED MY SHEEP

Whispering emotion
Where hope and the Kingdom of Heaven
Breathe with the Holy Breath
Of devotion.
And where God
Opens His Heart and says,
"Follow Me to feed my sheep.
And in feeding my sheep,
Eternity will touch the slumber
Of a sleeping man's soul
To bring him to the morning
Where a Master's arms, with grace,
Are open
To the bereavement of weeping innocence
Through to the sweeping joy
Of love expressed
Through the gentleness of devotion.

SWEET MEDITATIONS

O God! The Father of Light!
Christmas is Christ Mass
And the brilliant and sensitive act of prayer
Reaching upward
To the holy flow of water,
Baptizing the sacred songs
Of mystery.
I am united
With Divinity in my soul,
And through that peaceful marriage
There bloom flowers
That the hands of children grace,
And sweet meditations
That touch with perseverance
The rapture of O God!
The Light of the Father.

THE FORM OF CHRIST PRAYING

The color azure or cobalt
Gold or white
From the circle of the Sun
Is replete
With the vibration of God
In the context of the form of Christ
Praying
To exalt and glorify and convert
The body of the Christ
Through transfiguration.
Bringing to this form
A Light so bright and powerful
It shatters the concept that preceded the Light
To such a degree
That the kneeling figure of Christ in prayer
Was beatified and
"Made a light unto the world."

PRINCE OF INDIA

In my Father's mansion
Of the House of the rising sun,
The Lord from India knocked upon my door.
I opened my door
And found a Prince standing there.
Looking rather like the mystic saint
Of the House of India.
He said, "Open thy door
To hear the prayer of my soul."
I opened my door
And my soul flew to India
On the cherished wind
Of Lemuria.
The cross of Jerusalem
Became my staff,
And the staff of India
Became my joy.
"Thou shalt be born anew
In thy Father's Kingdom."

DANCES WITH FOXES

A trellis slipped on golden ground
Near a silver pond where children
Were playing
With ice.
Yet the bitterness of the cold
Couldn't touch the child near the Sun.
With apple wine caught in a tendril
That was lazy,
There moved within a sea of dreams
A new dream that wasn't idle or lazy.
The golden ground
Remembered the little foxes
Who lived in shanty homes
Next to the silver pond,
And the little foxes would touch the heart
Of the child next to the Sun and say,
"The cold is not bitter at the time of the Sun,
Yet the bitter is cold
At the setting of the sun."
Dances with foxes will bring forgiveness
If the fox is loved.
And if the fox is not loved,
A sigh will travel to Heaven for the unforgiven.

CHILD-WALK

Children walked on the rain
In rainbow-colored jackets
Carrying fresh blossoms of apples
That gazed at the Sun
Like mellow gospels of time
That were frayed at the edges.
The children,
Innocent in sweetness,
Not bitter or forsaken
Because their years in the Sun had been kind.
The children walked without hesitation
Where amber lightning flashed.
With the reverence of a child
Caught in the rain without a bonnet.

Fresh blossoms of apples
That were at once splendid and fragrant,
Like the Fragrance of the Father
Found the heart of the reverent child
Gazing at the Sun
With the remembrance of inspiration
That was so eloquent, yet intricate,
It cast spells in the desert.

TO LOVE HIM

To love Him who first loved us,
While flowers from Saint Mary's hands
Touch the hands of His children.
"Suffer the little children to come unto Me,
For the Kingdom of God
Belongs to such as these."
I spoke, Lord,
And as a child I looked at Him
Who loved us first,
And what I saw
Was emotion that was so rich,
So vivid,
It embraced Eternity from Heaven
With such outstanding Passion
That I said to my Lord with tears,
"May I hold your hand
While I walk to Heaven with you?"
I offered a cup of water in His name,
And immediately there rose
From the core of my being
The baptism of my soul.

A TRIBUTE TO PARAMAHANSA YOGANANDA

Yogananda,
Child of the Desert
And Child of the Sun,
Sent a smile to the Sun
That pierced the gold and left a
Teardrop of joy.
"This is my beloved son,"
Said the God of the Lamb,
And the Lamb of the Father
Relayed secrets of the desert
With musical tones
That smiled to the Child of the Sun.
His voice of song
Imbued with the power of the Holy Ghost
Fully embraced the Vibration of God
To produce tones that proclaimed
The Priest of India to be a Prophet of Gold.
In deep meditation,
Yogananda would contemplate
In the sleepless trance of the mystic,
And the slumberless thoughts of the Father
Would unravel blessings and love that were profound
In the year of the new books of the Kings.

A TRIBUTE TO STEVIE WONDER

Light of the lands of kings who wept
With silent rhapsody
At the feet of one who offered eternal salvation
To the innocent and the noble,
To the suffering and the wild.
The Light would pour from Heaven
In such immaculate abundance,
And through a prayer to the One
Would flow the tears of the righteous.
Mixed with gentleness the tears of the One.
A carpet of roses
Where nightingales with blue wings
That flew effortlessly and brilliantly
With the wind
Found at the fountain of the Holy Spirit
The crown of the singer,
Who stood there before another Crown
And felt merit pierce his soul
With eloquence
As a concert of energy
Swept through his entire Temple
Including the stage.
The Light before the anointed
Was sharp and as golden violet
As the midnight sky
Where the motion of the stars
Caused the Blue Rose of Sharon
To reach for a holy blue rose
To give to the star.

EMERALD TO GOLD, FOR A DOCTOR

There was a sovereign sign
That flew across the sky
When the sky was Golden
And flushed with the shade of rose.
There was a medical sign that was emerald
Upon which a young boy of virtue clasped his hands
And said, "My vow to God will be
Emerald to Gold.
The emerald shall be healing
Mixing with the Gold
So that I may heal!"
The sovereign sign sealed the Gold
And was in the shape of a cross.

TO AN ANGEL OF WISDOM

O Angel
Of the sapphire robes,
Like an Angel of wisdom
You seek council
With the Pearls of the Ocean of Mercy.
And the jewels you wear
Shimmer with the Light
Of the Radiant (Jesus).
You walk tall,
And touch roses,
And sing vespers in the evening
To Our Lady of Grace.
And she leans toward you
With an eternal rose
And says,
"O Angel of wisdom
Touch a rose that was
On the crucifix of Jesus
In the Valley of the Son (Calvary).
And the tears you weep
Will fall to other flowers,
And those flowers will weep, too.
And don't forget
The crown he wore,
A crown of thorns
That has echoed
Throughout the centuries.
"A King was born in Bethlehem!"
Whose Passion

Touched the skies
And they weep, too.
Excel, glorious, hallelujah!
On the wind lives tomorrow,
And by reason of sorrow
Not forgotten, but forgiven,
There'll be ecstasy
Which will bloom like a Rose of Sharon.

THE FIRST REAL ROSE OF ISRAEL

In the morning
Rests truth.
And the Power and Love
Of virtue Divine
Towers against the
Morning sky
Where there is the
Fire and the tears.
The tears stream
From the face
Of Christ.
And the fire
Erupted
From the hearts
Of the Apostles
Like the fire from a mountain
That would never
Stop weeping.
Saint John, the beloved Apostle, stood
Where roses bloomed.
And Saint Mary stood
At the foot of the cross
Where more roses bloomed.
And the Master Jesus said,
"John, this is now your mother," (meaning Mary).
And
"Mary, this is now your son," (meaning John).
The sun had eclipsed

Behind clouds that were dark
And the Sun,
Who was the Father,
Said,
"The Eternal Rose
Was born today,
And today the Rain
Began to fall."
And the first real rose
Of Israel
Bloomed at the base of the cross.

THE EVERLASTING MOUNTAINS

God in His immaculate Heaven
Looks down on the mountains of Canada
With so much love because the radiance
Of the Redeemer
Known through
The House of David
Was born in
The mountains of Israel.
Heart of Jesus,
Sacred Temple of God,
His words were these
As He taught on the mountain,
"Blessed are the merciful
For they will be shown mercy.
Blessed are the peacemakers,
For they are the children
Of the Radiance known as the Light,
And are also called the children
Of the Father."
Beloved, walk tall
Amongst the mountains
You love,
And feel the Power
And the mildness
Of the Beatitudes
Rush through your heart
Like a fountain of beauty.
And as you rest
In the hand of God,

May the Rose of Sharon
Bless you with petals
Of roses (which are the rosary)
Where the fragrance is so sweet, that,
Beloved of the Master,
May you always know
The Fragrance of the Father
And the Redolence of the rosary.

BLUEBIRDS FOREVER AND
THE GOLDEN STAR

The meadowlark
Of blue wing
Touched a Golden Star,
Then Yeshua ben Joseph
Was born
Through the mist
And the allure
Of all that was
Golden.
His sweet mother
Miriam (who is Mary)
Was born
Amidst lilies and roses.
And, one day,
An Angel called Gabriel said,
"Hail, full of grace."
The White Light of
The very Holy Spirit
Was around her,
And, of a day,
Her name became Bittersweet,
Which is the interpretation of Miriam.
The Grace of the Father (which is Mary)
And the Fountain of Beauty (which is Mary)
Loves everyone so very much,

Through the perfection of the Lamb
And through the rosary of the Rose of Nazareth.
Each person is blessed each day,
And through the glorification of Jesus
And the Assumption of the Virgin,
There is peace and joy.
If you ever see bluebirds,
Remember Bittersweet
Who wears a blue robe.
And when you see a Golden Star,
Remember Jesus, God-Man of Virtue,
And the Angels in Heaven
Will look upon each beautiful heart.
And, through the power of the rosary
And the nature of the Dove,
The Angels will say,
"You take my breath away!"

BEQUEATHED TO THY PERSON

Bequeathed to thy beauteous person
Are roses of the Rose of Nazareth.
And with flowers there are petals, and
From the treasury of grace are these words,
"O Mary, conceived without sin
Pray for us who have recourse to thee."
See the blue in the passionate skies
And the clouds that weep rain.
Remember the Valley of the Son (Calvary)
Where the air became dark
When the Son of Man, crucified,
Ascended as the Son of God.
And the rain poured vehemently
Throughout the darkness and the confusion
As the people wept and knew such sorrow.
Then the stone was taken away from the tomb
And there stood the Master Jesus,
An apparition of Light
Who gave the word Light as well
When He, as a vision of Gold, ascended to Heaven.
The Son, as born of God,
Who liveth in His children's beautiful heart
Has poured the gifts of the Holy Spirit
Upon each loving soul.
And through His love
Comes the grace of the Virgin,
"Hail Mary, full of grace."
Being without original sin and
Being the mother of God,

She yielded her heart
To great suffering.
Yet, as the Flower of Jerusalem,
The petals she offers each child of God
Are the petals of the rosary.
And maybe,
Petals will fall
To the feet of all children
As they recite the rosary,
The lingering scent of roses
Arising to Heaven
Which is each child's devotion to Mary.

WHISPER UNTO ETERNITY

The clouds that rise in a beautiful haven
Are touched
With the grace of the Son,
And the Flame of His Heart
Touches the Sun.
And the clouds carry with them
The color of rose.
The roses bloom
With lilies entwined.
It was with a lily
That Mary was betrothed
And with roses
That Queen Mary
Assumpted to Heaven,
"Hail Mary, full of grace."
Whisper unto Eternity
A rosary of Passion and light.
It's a meditation of devotion
To Sweet Mary
And a prayer of reflection
According to the Mysteries.
And according to the beauteous Gospel
That reflects in beauty and truth—
A Sermon on a Mountain.
"Go tell it on the mountain,
Over the hills and everywhere."

A ROSE ON AN ANGEL'S WING

There was a rose
That lingered
On an Angel's wing.
"Hail Mary, full of grace."
And even before the Angel arose to Heaven,
She clasped her hands around the world
And said, "Beautiful Saint Mary,
The Eternal Truth you represent,
The Savior, Earth's sanctification,
Has also known roses,
And, from the fervor in His soul
He's touched untold rosaries
And blessed them
In the convents and the churches
With the Holy Sacrament
Of His tears
Through His Passion."
The Angel said, "As I arise to heaven
Remember
The bitter ocean
Jesus found in Calvary,
Which ebbed away
As a lance touched
His Sacred Heart,
To become
The flowing rivers
Of Living Waters,
A powerful Ocean of Mercy."

Wings around the world
With a rose on an Angel's wing,
"Hail Mary, full of grace."

THE POWER OF GOLD

The sky is full of Gold,
The symbol of the stars.
Are we on a journey
Through life?
Or is it an odyssey?
The birds fly through Gold, too,
And the flowers grow through Gold
On each blossom
As all send their thoughts—
The power of words—
Through to the beauteous Cosmos
Of God,
From which Source we are all truly loved.
Roses have bloomed
Through Golden storms,
And blossoms have dropped
Through thorns on the stem.
"Hail Mary, full of grace."
The roses became
The flowers of forgiveness
Through the Immaculate Conception.
And remember the Son
Who walked in Light?

His words of Light
Went from the very centre of Earth
To the Golden Sun,
Then to the stars,
And then to Heaven
Where Angels wept
To behold Man as God, Golden,
And to hear His words of Love.
And may the Grace of God
Be with each child of God
Because life is an odyssey,
A jewel before the Father.

THE GIVING OF A FLOWER IN THE DESERT

The Rose of Sharon
Dropped a petal
And as it rested
In the desert of God,
There was a memory of a lily
That had an ambiance
Of purity and devotion.
Gather tears on the petals of the lily
When it was given in the desert
By Saint Joseph.
And as the the lily
Wept tears of astonishment,
So did the first petal
Of the rosary
Weep with bereavement
That became forgiveness.
And the children of Light
Were reborn through the Rose
And through the Radiance
As Spirit given through the Valley of the Son
That was finally understood
At the time of Emmaus.

FORGIVENESS WRITTEN THERE

The shining Light of God
Struck a raindrop in its centre
And the rain broke into smaller drops
That broke into Light as they touched the Sun.
The Son touched a drop of rain
That had touched the glorious Sun
And found forgiveness written there
By the God-Man who was the Son.
The begotten rain that had touched the Sun
Had also touched the Merciful Ocean.
Forgiveness was written thereby each begotten
Who had ever touched the Sun.

HE WHO WALKED WITH GOD

The rich scent of rain
Falls from the skies,
And the laughter of children
Peals across the Earth.
The Master Jesus walks barefoot
With crystals of sand dropping from his feet.
And when He taught the children,
Wild flowers tumbled from their hands.
As He was a Man of Goldenness.
Each word He said was uttered in Gold,
As He spoke parable after parable
And precious words about the Father.
And prisms on the Sea of Galilee
Where He walked on water
Shone and rippled with Light
Of the Son.
The Eternal Rose of Sharon,
"Fair as the moon, bright as the sun,"
Carries a Rosary of grace
For the children of Mary.
And the Radiance called the Lamb
Carries in His arms a lamb:
The eternal child of Christ.

A PRAYER IN THE TEMPLE

In that which is called
The Temple of Grace,
A Temple of God's sweet silence
Where the prayers of His children
Find their way
From the Temple of Silence
To the Temple of Grace, a church.
The Temple of Silence
Is humble and dear
In its silence,
Where the prayers to Jesus
Are rich in meaning
As they riot to Heaven
Through the white crown of God.
"Hail Mary, full of grace," and Light,
Bestow upon me this day
Compassion and love that are equal
To Jesus' beautiful compassion and Love
When He was on Earth.
And if it cannot be equal to,
Then, on my way to the Light
May I shine with the desire
To be like your Son.
Amen.

THE GOLDEN SHEPHERD

The Golden Shepherd,
The Messiah of God
Looked with eyes
That spoke of the mysteries of virtue
And of sorrow.
With eyes that wept
At the time of Lazarus,
"See how he loved him,"
To eyes that looked to Heaven
And to the consolation of an Angel of God
In the Garden of Gethsemane.
The words He spoke
Were words as these,
"The day is at hand"
And "Put on the armor of Light."
As the Golden Shepherd,
The gift of Light that He bears
Is so radiant
It brings tears to the eyes of His children,
Who in turn look with eyes
Where compassion is kindling,
And where Faith, Love, and Charity
Glow like burning embers of timelessness.

Amen! Amen! I say again,
The Radiance of the Gold Lamb
Sends teachings that are of Light
That are the signs of the Father,
And signs of the Son,
And signs of the Age.
As "Upon This Rock,"
Upon which a timeless Church was built.
Amen.

FROM THE DIVINE LIGHT

In the color of morning
That was fresh with the color of Spring
There was a woman
Who was having tea.
There was a statue of Jesus
Beside her favorite cup,
And there was a Bible
That told her:
"You are my beloved daughter,
And through the Divine and Immortal Light
That are from the wounds of my body
Came the healing and love of thy soul.
From the revelation
Of the Blood of the New Testament
Comes rushing with love
From the Fountain of my Mercy
The forgiveness from atonement
That is met with the baptism of thy soul.
Amen."

THE FACE OF THE FATHER

The rosary of the image
Of the sweet grace of the Divine
Echoes in its feeling
The image of the imageless.
In beautiful Heaven
The timeless Angels see
The face of the Father,
But that image is imageless.
While yet bearing a cross,
The walk through a valley
Called the Valley of the Son (Calvary)
Was known to the Father,
The imageless One.
And in the garden of Gethsemane
Where the Master truly wept
Tears and the sweat of Blood,
The sins of the people
Which were known to the Christ
Were truly forgiven
That day on the cross.

I worship and bless you,
Father who is without image
And whose face is dearly
Reflected in the countenance of His Son.
"Jesus, Temple of God, I love you so!"

A PRAYER TO SAINT JOSEPH

Saint Joseph, virgin father of Jesus,
Look down from whence thou art,
A shining star for us to see,
A shining star of such wealth
Of attributes:
Clemency, Truth, Virtue.
Our Solace and Protector and Restorer.
Thou with the light gold hair
With which the gaiety of the wind
Caresses with Love.
With a yellow robe
And carrying an amaryllis lily,
Which you gave to Mary, your betrothed,
In the desert.
Carpenter of Faith and Mercy
You build other Houses today,
And maybe thou buildeth mansions
In thy Father's House
With thy son, Jesus, in which,
"In my Father's House there are many mansions."
O Perfect Joseph,
Send us joy and discipline
That we may learn and grow,
May learn the lessons of thy son
And may we be perfected
By the forgiveness and love of the Lamb.
And may we walk with you, Joseph,
One day in the sun.

THE BEAUTIFUL CHRIST AND
THE BEAUTUFUL VIRGIN

The Flower of the Bible
Is the Fragrance of the Father
Whose name, in rapture, is Jesus.
In rapture, too, is the Flower of Jerusalem,
Saint Mary.
And the flowers of Mary
Bloomed a long time ago—
Queen of the Rose and Queen of Sharon—
They blossomed in Heaven where she was assumpted
And crowned, through the coronation of Mary.
Today, she weeps for her blessed children
As she did just yesterday,
But roses can bring rapture
To the Beautiful, the Virgin, in prayer.
The Fragrance of the Father
Gives from the Gates of Heaven
Learning from the hands of God,
How to bless and commit to memory
That Holy Fragrance.
The teaching is from the Fragrance of God,
What He taught before He died,
And when, at the time of Emmaus,
The Master's parables were finally understood.
And he lost His life to crucifixion,
And made His immaculate Ascension.
His apostles learned from the spirit of Christ.
Then they taught from His words

And from His acts
From whence He was glorified.
Jesus had said, "I am here to accomplish
My Father's work."
He also prayed, "That all may be one,
Even as Thou, Father,
In Me and I in Thee."
Saint Mary clasps her hands in prayer
And Jesus prays to God
(And He is the very Bouquet of the Father).

A TORCH OF LIGHT

By the lighting of a candle
By the law and the grace of the Lord
Walks Saint Mary,
Who is anointed by God.
And where, too, walks her son,
Christ, Head over all
Who is anointed
By the hand of God,
His Father.
"Our Father who art in Heaven."
We learned righteousness
By the grace of the Law,
And by grace alone
We learned forgiveness.
Let us walk with You,
Our Beloved Redeemer,
And let our love and faithfulness
Take us from the world
To a life of consecration.
A torch of Light left Heaven
When Jesus was born
That was powerful, potent, and eternal.
It was meant to be
The Light of the One God.
And for the Beautiful Saint Mary

There was a torch of Light
Lit from the stars
By the Beloved
That said, "World without end."
Amen.

AN ANGEL'S PRAYER FOR A CHILD

The Angel Gabriel prays for us
With hands clasped tightly to the Lord's
And the pure land of God
Rejoices when the names Mary or Jesus
Are pronounced.
And Heaven rejoices to touch thy beautiful hair, child.
The Fount of the Immaculate Conception
Flows over,
Till thy cup runneth over.
Angels touch Holy water
And put it on your brow
With so much love!
And may the trumpet of Joshua
Make a pleasant sound to your ear
As you listen to
The sweet voice of the Master.
And wild flowers filled with odor
Will drift from your rosary
To the Cosmic delight
Of those great beings
Called Angels.
They are on Earth to comfort you.

THE GARDEN

The weeping of the child
Who stood in the forests of India
Could be heard by the gentle Master.
With arms that were sweet and powerful
And robes that shone with light,
He enfolded the child in his arms.
And what passed from grace to silence
Was love that was pure and direct.
In the Silence of Grace
He said, "Child, you will know sorrow,
But it will leave a flower in your heart
That will give rise to another flower,
A flower of ecstasy."
The child shivered in the night air.
The first flower could have thorns.
Then the child wept yet on another day
Experiencing total ecstasy.

VICTORY OF THE ROSES

The Victory of the Roses
Was certain in the year 2001.
Saint Anne gave her prayer to her daughter, Mary,
As the snow lay pure on the ground.
And when Saint Mary, her beloved child, was born,
She prayed again for the love of humankind.
Then, in the year 2001, Saint Anne came to a saint
Who was Holy,
Who was a saint of the Lord
And said, "Child of God,
The love of Jesus and my daughter,
Who was born without original sin,
Is written upon thy brow.
The cross is known to thee,
Not only in the silence of grace,
But in the grace of the Law of God.
You are adorned in the clothes of the Law,
And thy love of Saint Mary and little Jesus
Is known to the Father."
Carrying roses and fire,
The saint released from her soul
A sweet dove who went to the Heavens
Who said, as the Holy Vibration of God
Touched and inflamed her spirit,
"This is my beloved daughter."
The Victory of the Roses,

Hallowed to the Lord
As, thorns upon the stem,
Left triumph throughout the land.
And the roses became like a cross.
But the aroma of the petals
Climbed all the way to Heaven
And reached the Gold that nestled there
With love, with grace, and with fire.

THE RAYS OF LIGHT

The mountains were born
As the oceans were made
And the Prophets gave words
Before Jesus was born.
Jesus, who had the voice of falling rain waters,
Rose like a white swan of David
In the city of Israel
Known as Jerusalem,
With roses pouring from His hands.
And from His golden hair
There were rays of light
That cascaded through the Heavens,
And the rays of light
Had issued forth from His Father,
And poured throughout the Earth
Like the many voices of the rain.
The power of the dove
Whose white wings had whirred
With the Spirit of Grace
At the time of the Baptist,
Had whirred with the accompaniment
Of a loud voice
That pierced the air, that said
"This is my Beloved Son."
As the brilliant light and the brilliant rain
Continued to flow through the world,
The white swan of David
Arose like a sword.
Merciful, just, and made of fire,

It cleaved Israel in two.
His apostles,
Drenched by light and by rain,
Had ears that heard.
And by the nature of the Dove
The Church Magnificent was born.

WARRIORS OF JUDAH

As the love poured through Autumn roses
And swept petals to the feet of the Blessed Virgin
She said, "My Heart of the Immaculate Rose
Carries four white roses of Christ
For the warriors of Judah."
The warriors stood tall and strong
And carried with them a sword of fire
That cleaved in two
The falseness and the ignorance
Of the untaught, who were in sin.
Blazing with the emblem of the Cross of Triumph
Carried in hands that were pure,
The warriors of Judah led an army of fire
Throughout the world,
And brought the heathen and publicans
To the Mirror of Justice (which is God).
And through the fire burned embers of faith
That were so very timeless and appropriate
To the Prince of Heaven, Jesus.
And the warriors of Judah
Venerated the Ten Commandments.
The Virgin of Victory and the Prince of Triumph
Who knew conquest at the time of Emmaus,
And, who through seven horses and chariots,
Became rulers and riders with the Sun.

YOUNG DAVID, YOUNG JESUS

David, a shepherd of Israel
Stood humbly
With tousled red hair.
A comely youth,
With songs gushing from his harp
And psalms rushing from his soul.
It is said that the prophet Samuel
Had filled his cup with oil
And went to the city
Known as Bethlehem.
There, seven of Jesse's sons
Had passed before him.
The prophet Samuel did not select one
Of these seven sons
To become the King of Israel,
But the eighth child was in the fields,
And this child became anointed,
And the Spirit of the Lord came upon him
Who was called by name, David.
After David's anointment, came a time
When there was war between Philistine and Israel.
A Philistine man stood on a mountain
Who was nine foot tall, and armored,
But not armored of the light.
David, astonished and offended,
Said, "Who is he who should taunt
The armies of the Living God?"

He also said, "When they came and took a lamb
From the flock
I went out after the lamb."
Thus,
David prospered in all ways
Because the Lord was with him.
Jesus, Son of the Living God,
Who was born in Bethlehem
Stood humbly
As a beloved youth
Gone from Jerusalem
And into beloved India,
A young male.
His hair was golden
And he wore robes of beauty
And of a normal appearance for his times.
When he was teaching
He was known as Saint Issa,
And he was received into India as a prophet.
His revelation of the Word
Came to him as a young man
And took the form of parables,
"I am the good shepherd
As the Father knows me,
And I know the Father,
I know my sheep and they know me,
And I give them everlasting life.
I and the Father are one."
His song was the song of the Father,
And his teachings rushed from his soul
With truth and with grace,

Like the Psalms of the Anointed.
And it was with humility and grace
That he stood tall
Before Pilate
And answered as a God.
And he lay his life down for his sheep.
And the man Pilate was armored,
But not armored in the light.
Jesus said to His brethren,
"I am the way, and the truth, and the life."
He also said, "And the glory
That thou hast given to me, Father,
I have given to my brethren."

CPSIA information can be obtained
at www.ICGtesting.com
Printed in the USA
LVOW04*0331080416
482691LV00001B/1/P